MW01592611

WORKBOOK

FOR

Quiet Your Mind and Get to Sleep

A Practical Guide on: Solutions to Insomnia for Those with Depression, Anxiety, or Chronic Pain.

HEATH PRINT

TABLE OF CONTENT

HOW TO USE THE WORKBOOK

Welcome! You've made the right choice by picking up this companion workbook for "Quiet Your Mind and Get to Sleep: Solutions to Insomnia for Those with Depression, Anxiety, or Chronic Pain" by Colleen E. Carney, PhD, and Rachel Manber, PhD. This workbook has been carefully designed to enrich your understanding and maximize your utilization of the original book. Our goal is to ensure you don't miss a single point and can fully digest every detail. Allow me to guide you on how to make the most of this workbook:

1. **Start with the Overview:** Begin by reviewing the overview or summary of the original book, which is provided chapter by chapter. This will give you a comprehensive understanding of the core concepts presented in the book.

2. **Explore Core Lessons:** As you delve into each chapter, you'll find core lessons that distill the key insights and takeaways. Take your time to absorb these lessons as they lay the foundation for your journey through the book's content.

3. **Reflect with Self-Introspection Questions:** After each set of core lessons, you'll encounter self-introspection questions. These questions are designed to encourage self-reflection and personal growth. Approach them with an open mind and be honest with yourself.

4. **Track Your Progress:** Feel free to jot down your thoughts and answers to the self-introspection questions within this workbook. This will help you track your progress and gain a deeper insight into your personal development.

5. **Use the Self-Evaluation Questions:** Towards the end of this companion workbook, you'll find a section with self-evaluation questions. This is your opportunity to assess your overall journey through the original book and the companion workbook.

6. **Apply What You Learn:** The most crucial step is to apply the knowledge and insights you gain from this workbook to your daily life. Use the strategies, techniques, and self-reflection to improve your sleep and well-being.

SUMMARY/OVERVIEW

Quiet Your Mind and Get to Sleep: Solutions to Insomnia for Those with Depression, Anxiety, or Chronic Pain by Colleen E. Carney, PhD, and Rachel Manber, PhD, is an extensive and insightful book that tackles the intricate relationship between sleep, mental health, and chronic pain. In this two-page summary, we aim to provide a comprehensive overview of the book's core concepts and how it can be a valuable resource in your journey towards better sleep and overall well-being.

This book is a substantial work, filled with invaluable insights that can significantly impact your life. Its thorough content is a treasure trove of wisdom, and every sentence and chapter holds a crucial point that you need to grasp to truly appreciate the book's ideas and context.

The Modern Dilemma: In our fast-paced, busy lives, characterized by long working hours and packed schedules, we often neglect the need for rest and relaxation. The relentless pursuit of success often leads to a lack of vacations and increased stress, ultimately making insomnia the number-one health problem in Western societies. Insomnia, in its essence, requires disengagement from the relentless pace of our environment, which is disrupted by stress in its various forms.

Insomnia and Mental Health: Insomnia is frequently accompanied by other health problems, including depression, anxiety, and chronic pain conditions. These coexisting issues can bring considerable personal suffering, along with the added burden of medication costs and doctor's appointments. Yet, traditionally, doctors didn't typically treat comorbid insomnia, assuming it would resolve once the primary condition was addressed. However, untreated comorbid insomnia often persists or worsens, negatively impacting the overall health of individuals.

Cognitive-Behavioral Therapy (CBT) for Insomnia: The book introduces an effective treatment for insomnia known as Cognitive-Behavioral Therapy (CBT). CBT is a well-established method used for various mental disorders, and it has been tested extensively for insomnia treatment. It is proven to be as effective as sleep medications, and most importantly, the benefits of CBT for insomnia tend to last longer, making it an ideal choice for individuals dealing with insomnia alongside other medical or mental conditions.

Tailored Recommendations: The book provides practical advice, specifically tailored for individuals facing insomnia alongside other health problems. It addresses common challenges such as managing anxiety, coping with low energy, and dealing with an overactive mind. The book recognizes that each person's struggles are unique and offers guidance to address individual challenges.

A Resource for All: "Quiet Your Mind and Get to Sleep" is a resource for anyone who has ever grappled with insomnia, as well as those who care about them. It helps individuals understand the underlying causes of insomnia and equips them with strategies to overcome it.

Medications and Treatment: If you are currently taking medication for sleep, pain, anxiety, or depression, the book's approach can still be effective. It provides guidance for using the strategies alongside medication. It's essential not to stop taking prescribed medications without consulting your physician, as abrupt discontinuation can be uncomfortable and potentially dangerous. It is crucial to continue getting treatment for coexisting conditions while addressing insomnia.

A Personal Journey: This approach allows for personal choices in making health-related changes. While the book is designed for self-help, you can also seek the assistance of a sleep specialist in your area. The goal is to empower you to take control of your insomnia by making small changes in your sleep routine and mindset.

The Scope of the Insomnia Problem

Key Lessons

1. **Understanding the Prevalence of Insomnia**: Learn about the prevalence of insomnia in those suffering from depression, anxiety, or chronic pain.

2. **The Relationship between Insomnia and Mental Health**: Discover the deep relationship between insomnia and disorders such as sadness and anxiety.

3. **The Effects of Chronic Pain on Sleep**: Learn how chronic pain can interrupt your sleep patterns and negatively impact your general well-being.

4. **Recognizing the Physical and Psychological Consequences:** Learn about the physical and psychological effects of chronic insomnia in the context of other health conditions.

5. **Obstacles to obtaining Help:** Identify typical barriers that may hinder people from obtaining help for their insomnia-related concerns.

SELF-REFLECTION QUESTIONS

1. How does your experience with insomnia compare to the chapter's prevalence?

----

2. Have you observed a link between your mental health and your sleep quality? If so, how does it affect your day-to-day life?

3. How has chronic pain affected your capacity to sleep well, and how does this affect your general well-being?

----

4. Consider the physical and psychological repercussions of your sleeplessness in the context of your medical problems. Is there anything in particular that has had a major influence on you?

----

5. Think about the obstacles described in the chapter that may be keeping you from obtaining assistance for your sleeplessness. What challenges have you faced, and how may you overcome them in order to enhance your sleep and general health?

Learning about Your Sleep

Key Lessons

1. Understanding Sleep Cycles: Learn about the complexity of the sleep cycle, from light sleep to deep sleep and REM sleep, in order to obtain insight into your own sleep habits.

2. Sleep Efficiency: Investigate the notion of sleep efficiency, learning how to calculate it and what it indicates about your sleep quality.

3. Recognizing Sleep Disruptors: Learn about typical sleep disruptors including coffee, technology, and irregular sleep schedules, as well as how they may impair your sleep.

4. Sleep Pattern Tracking: Learn how to keep a sleep diary to monitor your sleeping habits and identify trends that may be contributing to sleep difficulties.

5. The Relationship Between Emotions and Sleep: Learn how emotions and stress may affect your sleep and how to manage these aspects to enhance your sleep quality.

SELF-REFLECTION QUESTIONS

1. How well do you understand your sleep cycles, and can you identify which stage you may be having the greatest difficulty with?

---

2. Have you calculated your sleep efficiency, and what does it say about your sleep's effectiveness?

----

3. What are the most prevalent sleep disruptors in your nighttime routine, and how can they be hurting your sleep quality?

----

4. Do you keep a sleep journal to document your sleeping patterns? Have you seen any recurring trends or causes for sleep disturbances?

----

5. Have you investigated the relationship between your emotions and sleep, and what tactics do you employ to handle stress and emotions that affect your sleep?

Understanding Insomnia and Your Sleep System

Key Lessons

1. The Sleep-Wake Cycle Learn about your body's natural sleep-wake mechanism and how it affects your sleep habits.

2. Recognize the role of worry and stress in disrupting your sleep system and contributing to insomnia.

3. Cognitive and Behavioral aspects: Investigate the cognitive and behavioral aspects, such as rumination and negative thought patterns, that might contribute to insomnia.

4. Sleep Hygiene and Environment: Discover how improving your sleep environment and following proper sleep hygiene may improve your sleep quality.

5. The Importance of Consistency: Learn the importance of sticking to a constant sleep pattern and the function it plays in controlling your sleep system.

SELF-REFLECTION QUESTIONS

1. How well do you understand your body's natural sleep-wake mechanism, and how does it affect your sleep patterns?

----

2. Have you recognized the precise concerns and stressors in your life that you believe are contributing to your sleeplessness, and how can you address them?

----

3. Are you aware of any cognitive or behavioral habits that may be sustaining your insomnia, such as rumination or negative thinking, and what steps you may take to change them?

----

4. How can you enhance your sleep environment and practice greater sleep hygiene to create a sleep-friendly atmosphere?

----

5. Do you have a consistent sleep routine, and if not, how can you build one in order to better regulate your sleep system and increase your sleep quality?

Sleep-Incompatible Behaviors: Tools for Change

Key Lessons

1. Recognize Sleep-Incompatible Behaviors: Recognize the actions and habits that interfere with your capacity to sleep well. Excessive screen time, unpredictable sleep cycles, or the ingestion of coffee or alcohol before bedtime are examples.

2. Recognize the Impact: Recognize how sleep-incompatible habits can increase insomnia, particularly in individuals suffering from despair, anxiety, or chronic pain. Recognize that modifying these patterns can lead to better sleep.

3. Establish a Sleep-Friendly Environment: Make changes to your sleeping environment to encourage healthier sleep. Adjust aspects such as room temperature, lighting, and noise to make your bedroom a more restful environment.

4. Create a Consistent Sleep Schedule: Create a consistent sleep schedule by going to bed and getting up at the same times every day, including on weekends. Consistency can aid in the regulation of your body's internal clock and the improvement of your sleeping habits.

5. Use Mindfulness and Relaxation Techniques: Learn and use relaxation techniques such as deep breathing, meditation, or progressive muscle relaxation to reduce stress and anxiety, which can lead to sleep issues.

SELF-REFLECTION QUESTIONS

1. Have you identified any specific activities that you believe are interfering with your ability to sleep well?

----

2. How do sleep-incompatible habits effect your sleep, particularly if you suffer from depression, anxiety, or chronic pain?

----

3. Have you taken any measures to make your bedroom a sleep-friendly environment?

----

4. Do you keep a regular sleep routine, going to bed and getting up at the same times every day?

5. Have you included mindfulness and relaxation strategies into your daily routine to assist manage stress and worry, which may be interfering with your sleep?

Optimizing Your Sleep System by Changing Your Habits

Key Lessons

1. Recognize the Influence of Routine: Creating a consistent sleep pattern may dramatically enhance your sleep quality. Do you prioritize a consistent sleep-wake cycle in your everyday life?

2. Limiting Stimulants and Electronics: Limiting caffeine and screen time before bedtime will help you relax and sleep better. Are you conscious of your stimulant consumption and screen usage in the hours before bedtime?

3. Establishing a peaceful nighttime routine: Establishing a peaceful nighttime routine helps indicate to your body that it is time to sleep. What relaxing activities do you include in your evening routine?

4. Stress and Anxiety Management: Addressing stress and anxiety with relaxation techniques might help you sleep better. How do you deal with stress now, and may you benefit from new techniques?

5. Improving Your Sleep Environment: Making your sleeping environment comfy, cool, and dark can improve your sleep quality. Have you made any changes to your sleeping environment to encourage better sleep?

SELF-REFLECTION QUESTIONS

1. Do you have a constant sleep pattern, and if not, how can you make a regular sleep-wake cycle a priority in your life?

----

2. How effectively do you manage your coffee consumption and screen time before bedtime, and what efforts can you take to minimize its effects on your sleep?

----

3. What are your present nighttime routines, and how successful are they in helping you unwind before bed? Are there any other relaxing activities you may include?

----

4. Consider your stress-management skills. Are they effective in reducing anxiety, or do you need to look into different relaxation and stress-reduction techniques?

----

5. Examine your sleeping surroundings. Is it favorable to good sleep? If not, what modifications can you do to create a more comfortable, cool, and dark sleeping environment?

Quieting Your Mind: Tools for Change

Key Lessons

1. Recognize the Power of Mindfulness: Recognize the importance of mindfulness in quieting your thoughts and promoting relaxation before going to bed.

2. Use Thought-Labeling Techniques: Learn how to successfully identify and control intrusive thoughts in order to keep them from developing into sleep-disrupting concerns.

3. Develop a Pre-Sleep Ritual: Create a pre-sleep ritual that signals to your mind and body that it's time to unwind and prepare for restful sleep.

4. Create a Worry Period: Schedule a worry period throughout the day to address problems, enabling your mind to rest reasonably soundly at night.

5. Practice Cognitive Restructuring: Use cognitive restructuring to challenge negative thinking patterns and establish a more pleasant and serene mental environment conducive to better sleep.

SELF-REFLECTION QUESTIONS

1. How can you successfully incorporate mindfulness into your everyday routine to relieve pre-sleep tension and calm your mind?

----

2. What thought-labeling strategies can you use to regulate intrusive thoughts and keep them from interfering with your sleep?

----

3. How can you create a tailored pre-sleep routine that fits your lifestyle and helps you relax before going to bed?

----

4. Have you developed a designated concern period during the day, and how can you guarantee that it successfully reduces pre-sleep anxiety?

----

5. What tactics can you use to confront and modify negative thinking patterns in order to develop a more pleasant and soothing mental state conducive to restful sleep?

When Thinking about Sleep Gets in the way of Sleep

Key Lessons

1. Recognize the Vicious Cycle: Recognize that excessive sleep anxiety may become a self-fulfilling prophesy, increasing anxiety and making it difficult to fall asleep.

2. Reframe unpleasant Thoughts: Learn to recognize and confront unpleasant sleep thoughts, and replace them with more positive and helpful ones.

3. Use Relaxation Techniques: To quiet your thoughts and lessen sleep-related worry, try relaxation activities such as deep breathing or progressive muscle relaxation.

4. Create a Consistent Sleep pattern: To assist regulate your body's internal clock, create an organized nighttime pattern that includes consistent wake and sleep hours.

5. Limit Stimulants and Screens Before Bed: To enhance sleep quality, limit or eliminate coffee consumption and the usage of electronic devices before bedtime.

SELF-REFLECTION QUESTIONS

1. Have you ever noticed how stressing about sleep interferes with your capacity to sleep?

----

2. What are your negative sleep ideas or beliefs, and how do they affect your sleep quality?

----

3. Can you think of any specific relaxation practices that can help you with sleep-related anxiety?

----

4. How consistent is your sleep regimen, and what modifications can you make to get back on track?

----

5. What stimulants or electronic gadgets do you use before going to bed, and how can restricting them help your sleep patterns?

Issues with Substances and Medications

Key Lessons

1. Recognize the Impact: Recognize how drugs and prescriptions affect your sleep quality and general well-being.

2. Evaluating Your Habits: Examine your current drug and medication use to discover potential sleep disruptors.

3. Investigating Alternatives: Look for healthy alternatives to drugs or prescriptions that may be interfering with your sleep.

4. Seek Professional Help: If you are concerned about the consequences of your substance or medicine usage on your sleep, seek advice from a healthcare expert or therapist.

5. Making Changes: To enhance your sleep patterns, take proactive efforts to adjust your behaviors and make educated decisions about drugs and prescriptions.

SELF-REFLECTION QUESTIONS

1. Recognizing the Impact: Do you understand how the drugs or medications you take may be influencing your sleep and general mental health?

----

2. Evaluating Your Habits: Have you assessed your current drug and medicine intake and its potential influence on your sleep?

----

3. Investigating Alternatives: Have you thought about healthy alternatives to drugs or pharmaceuticals that may be interfering with your sleep patterns?

---

4. Seeking Professional Help: Have you sought the advice of a healthcare practitioner or therapist regarding any concerns you may have about your substance or medication usage and its influence on your sleep?

----

5. Change Implementation: What measures are you actively taking to change your behaviors and make better educated decisions about drugs and prescriptions to improve your sleep quality?

When things get in the way of Treatment

Key Lessons

1. Recognize Your Sleep Obstacles: Recognize the precise causes that prevent you from falling asleep, such as stress, bad thoughts, or physical discomfort.

2. Creating a Support Network: Recognize the significance of obtaining help from friends, family, or healthcare experts to address the issues associated with insomnia and its link to depression, anxiety, or chronic pain.

3. Establishing a Consistent Routine: Maintain a regular sleep schedule and use relaxation methods to encourage better sleep quality, especially if you are struggling with mental health concerns.

4. Cognitive-Behavioral Strategies: Discover how to use cognitive-behavioral approaches to regulate intrusive thoughts and increase sleep, while concentrating on your mind's ability to overcome barriers.

5. Being adaptable and devoted: Be adaptable in your approach to therapy and remain devoted to treating the underlying reasons of your insomnia, even if you face setbacks or unpleasant situations.

SELF-REFLECTION QUESTIONS

1. Have you discovered the precise variables that routinely interfere with your ability to fall asleep, and how can you solve them?

----

2. Have you sought help from friends, relatives, or healthcare experts for sleeplessness, particularly if it is associated with sadness, anxiety, or chronic pain?

----

3. Do you maintain a consistent sleep regimen and use relaxation techniques to improve the quality of your sleep, especially while dealing with mental health issues?

----

4. How can you use cognitive-behavioral tactics to minimize intrusive thoughts and enhance your sleep patterns while also acknowledging the impact of your perspective on conquering obstacles?

----

5. Are you prepared to change your treatment method as needed and remain devoted to resolving the underlying reasons of your insomnia, even if you face setbacks or difficult circumstances?

SELF-EVALUATION QUESTIONS

1. Have you actively used the book's concepts and procedures to solve your insomnia and related issues?

----

2. Based on the book's recommendations, what particular adjustments have you made in your daily routine, sleep habits, or thought patterns, and how have they influenced your sleep quality?

----

3. Have you enlisted the help of others, such as friends, family, or healthcare experts, in your quest to enhance your sleep and mental health?

----

4. How effectively have you recognized and treated the issues that may be interfering with your sleep, especially those connected to depression, anxiety, or chronic pain?

---

5. Are you more aware of the relationship between your mental health and sleep habits, and have you made actions to remedy it?

----

6. How far have you progressed in implementing cognitive-behavioral methods to decrease intrusive thoughts and promote better sleep?

----

7. Have you kept a consistent sleep pattern and used relaxation techniques as indicated in the book?

----

8. How have you altered your treatment strategy and remained motivated to overcoming barriers on your journey to improved sleep?

----

9. Have you noticed any improvements in your sleep quality or overall well-being since starting the book?

----

10. How do you intend to continue utilizing the book's concepts in your life in the future to maintain and enhance your sleep and mental health?

Made in United States
Cleveland, OH
04 January 2025

13082678R00046